Ernest Hemingway's

A FAREWELL TO ARMS

A CRITICAL COMMENTARY

LAWRENCE KLIBBE
PROFESSOR OF ROMANCE LANGUAGES
NEW YORK UNIVERSITY

NOTE:
THIS GUIDE IS INTENDED TO SUPPLEMENT AND ENHANCE THE ORIGINAL WORK OF ART.

Published by
MONARCH PRESS
a Simon & Schuster division of
Gulf & Western Corporation
Simon & Schuster Building
1230 Avenue of the Americas
New York, N.Y. 10020

Standard Book Number: 0-671-00671-1

Library of Congress Catalog Card Number: 65-7244

Printed in the United States of America

CONTENTS

INTRODUCTION

Ernest Hemingway soared to literary and financial success after the publication of *A Farewell To Arms* in 1929. Although *The Sun Also Rises* (1926) brought him a great deal of critical recognition, this novel did not strike the immediate response in the public's heart which *A Farewell To Arms* did. That book sold 80,000 copies in four months. Hemingway entered the limelight of popularity, and the problem arose of distinguishing between the artist, the legend, and the man.

EARLY LIFE: He was born on July 21, 1899 in Oak Park, Illinois, a small, middle-class suburb of Chicago. Nothing in his early background indicated the bold approach he was to employ in his novels. The second of six children, Hemingway led the normal, active life of a schoolboy. Although not especially popular, he took part in sports, debates, the school orchestra, wrote and edited the school newspaper. Summers were spent outdoors in northern Michigan at a family camp. However, tensions evidently existed between the parents. Dr. Clarence E. Hemingway, a physician and enthusiastic outdoorsman, instilled in the young Ernest a love of hunting, fishing, and the natural life which he never abandoned. Grace Hall Hemingway, very pious and very active in church affairs, tried to interest the son in music and cultural pursuits; for example, Ernest was taught to play the cello. The young Hemingway ran away from home twice, and worked at a number of odd jobs. His chance at escape from family and small-town pressures came when the United States entered World War I in 1917. He immediately volunteered but was rejected because of an eye injury; however, he was accepted as an ambulance driver on the Italian front early in 1918.

WORLD WAR I: Hemingway's experiences in the first World War fashioned much of his personal and literary outlook. After leaving his job as a reporter on the *Kansas City Star* to join the ambulance corps in Italy, he was abruptly and brutally introduced to the facts of war. He witnessed a munitions explosion in Milan upon his arrival, and on July 8, 1918, just before his nineteenth birthday, he was severely wounded. He underwent twelve operations for removal of some two hundred fragments of mortar shell but returned to the war as an infantry officer with the Italian Army. Two medals were awarded Hemingway by the Italian Government for his bravery during World War I. These experiences are vividly reflected in *A Farewell To Arms*. His hero Frederic Henry depicts the whole attitude of Hemingway toward war and men at war.

THE TWENTIES: The restlessness of Hemingway in the period between the end of World War I and the publication of *A Farewell To Arms* became apparent in his many and varied activities during these ten years. He married Hadley Richardson in 1921 but they were divorced in 1927. Hemingway married Pauline Pfeiffer, to whom he dedicated *A Farewell To Arms,* the same year. He worked for the Toronto *Star* and *Star Weekly* from 1920 until 1924. In 1921 he returned to Europe and traveled widely throughout the continent. He fell in love with Spain, which figures so prominently in his writings, during the twenties. He covered the Greco-Turkish War, and the Greek retreat from Smyrna may be a model for the Italian debacle of Caporetto, portrayed in *A Farewell To Arms*. Hemingway also covered the international events of that decade and met such world figures as Lloyd George, Clemenceau, and Mussolini. Hemingway early grasped the dangers of Fascism and wrote scathingly of the Italian dictator, whom he disliked immediately. In 1924 Hemingway settled in Paris to devote himself to his own writing and was introduced through Sherwood Anderson to the influential circle of Gertrude Stein. Meanwhile, his stories had started to appear in such magazines as *Atlantic Monthly*. He published *Three Stories And Ten Poems* in 1923; *In Our Time,* a compendium of stories and vignettes, in 1924; the expanded version of these Nick Adams stories, *In Our Time*, in 1925, in the United States; *The Torrents of Spring,* a satirical, unsuccessful novel, in 1926; and of course, *The Sun Also Rises,* in 1926, and *A Farewell To Arms,* in 1929. His father's suicide in 1928 affected him greatly.

THE THIRTIES: Hemingway's reputation mounted during these years. He traveled a great deal, which is reflected in the work of that period. He published thirty-one articles and stories in *Esquire; Death In The Afternoon* in 1932 and *Winner Take Nothing* in 1933; and *The Green Hills Of Africa* in 1935. When the Spanish Civil War broke out in 1936, Hemingway went to Spain as a correspondent for the North American Newspaper Alliance. His sympathies were on the side of the Loyalists against the forces of Franco. In 1937 he published the novel *To Have And Have Not.* In 1938 he published *The Fifth Column and the First Forty-Nine Stories*—a volume containing the title play, and all the stories of his previous collections, in addition to seven published but uncollected tales. In 1940 he published *For Whom The Bell Tolls,* a novel about the Spanish Civil War, which had great success. He was divorced again that year and immediately married Martha Gellhorn.

LATER LIFE: Hemingway eagerly looked forward to action in World War II. He maintained an anti-submarine patrol in Cuban waters and planned to decoy submarines with his own boat. Obviously restless in Cuba, where he had settled after 1940, Hemingway went again as a war correspondent to France where he organized a group of irregulars. He entered Paris among the first, in August of 1944, and "liberated" the Ritz Hotel, where he posted a guard with the notification: "Papa took good hotel. Plenty stuff in cellar." His third marriage ended in divorce in 1944 and he married Mary Welsh. "Papa" Hemingway had three children of his early marriages: John by the first, Patrick and Gregory by the second. After the war, Hemingway published *Across The River And Into The Trees,* a novel about World War II, which was bitterly attacked by the critics. However, in 1952, he published *The Old Man And The Sea,* a story generally acclaimed one of his finest. He survived an airplane crash in 1954, the year he received the Nobel Prize in Literature. But his injuries had taken their toll and Hemingway died of a "self-inflicted gunshot wound" on July 2, 1961, in his home at Ketchum, Idaho.

A FAREWELL TO ARMS: Besides providing Ernest Hemingway with financial security and a vast reading public in the United States and overseas, *A Farewell To Arms* expressed in poignant terms the concept of Hemingway's art and ideas. The President of the Swedish Academy, upon awarding him the Nobel Prize in literature in 1954, summed up the contributions which are so clearly expounded in *A Farewell To Arms*: ". . . a heroic pathos which forms the basic element in his awareness of life . . . a natural admiration of every individual who fights the good fight in a world of reality overshadowed by violence and death . . . the bearing of one who is put to the test and who steels himself to meet the cold cruelty of existence without by so doing repudiating the great and generous moments . . . He is one of the great writers of our time, one of those who, honestly and undauntedly, reproduces the genuine features of the hard countenance of the age."

THE WAR YEARS: The age which Hemingway depicts so vividly in *A Farewell To Arms* is the period of 1914-1918 when European civilization suffered a severe jolt to its ideals in the "circus of death." For almost one hundred years, since Napoleon's defeat at Waterloo and the Congress of Vienna in 1815, Europe had been comparatively peaceful. Although nationalism had produced troublesome rivalries, the European powers concentrated on building their economies at home as well as in their colonies. At the beginning of the war, a quick victory according to traditional methods of warfare was the hope of all the warring powers; but soon the monotonous death of trench warfare and the mounting casualties in senseless attacks and counterattacks destroyed the dream of a short war. Propaganda appealed not only to patriotic motives, such as the defense of the fatherland, but also to more noble ideals, such as a crusade to protect culture. As the United States was dragged inexorably closer and closer to entry into the war, American men volunteered for service in Europe.

Frederic Henry, in *A Farewell To Arms,* learned that the individual mattered little in this widening world conflict. Personal courage and manliness were useless against machines; masses of troops were transferred at will from section to section; mismanagement by the generals, ignorant of the new type of fighting, destroyed trust and bred cynicism; and the general corruption, common in all wars, increased as the fighting dragged on. In such a confused, mass-scale war of four years costing ten million casualties, one person mattered little. Thus, idealism and patriotism became hollow concepts. This universal malaise endured throughout the next decade. A general revulsion toward war was bred, which helps to explain some of Hemingway's success with *A Farewell To Arms.* In 1929, the novel exactly reflected American and European attitudes toward World War I.

The soldiers expressed a similar disgust at the 1914-1918 sacrifices even if they had not suffered as extensively as Hemingway's hero. The nineteen-twenties have been dubbed the age of "the lost generation," and Hemingway, who sketched some of the expatriates in *The Sun Also Rises,* explains in *A Farewell To Arms* why youth sought refuge in pleasure and refused to adjust to the demands of the nineteen-twenties. It is clear at the end of the novel that Frederic Henry, like so many young men, has suffered in vain; his efforts have had no bearing on the struggle; his whole service has been wasted on an absurdity; and he has lost the chance to find love and happiness. He is doomed to wander from sensation to sensation, matured but embittered by his terrible experiences.

THE AUTOBIOGRAPHICAL: Every writer must draw upon his own experiences and the adventures of Hemingway are apparent in *A Farewell To Arms.* For example, he reported in the nineteen-twenties the Greek defeat and retreat at Smyrna at the hands of the Turks; and though he arrived in Italy after the disastrous Caporetto retreat, he undoubtedly heard many tales about it and read reports in the newspapers. The shock of war was brought home when he helped in the munitions explosion episode in Milan very shortly after his arrival in Italy. This traumatic episode was reinforced by his own brush with death in 1918 when he was hospitalized after being severely wounded. The experience is quite similar to that of Frederic Henry in the first book of the novel. Hemingway saw in action and in war an outlet for his emotions and thoughts. He became a more active combatant after returning to the front in 1918, transferring to the infantry, and fighting until the armistice with the Italians. Later, in Paris, Hemingway recalled his difficulties in setting down in writing what he experienced: "I was trying to write, and I found that my greatest difficulty (apart from that of knowing what you truly felt, rather than what you were supposed to feel, or what you had been taught to feel) was to note what really happened in action, what the actual things were which produced the emotion which you experienced . . . I was trying to learn to write, commencing with the simplest things." *A Farewell To Arms* is a novel with such a strong autobiographical element (which does not detract from its creative and imaginative power) that it supplied much of the foundation for the "Hemingway Cult."

THE HEMINGWAY CULT: Hemingway in many ways deliberately sought an extension of the "Hemingway Cult" and fostered in his travels and adventures the idea. According to the code of Hemingway, Frederic Henry must reject all complex and rarefied thought and philosophy; he must see everything in terms of the simple and elementary. He is not afraid of death, faces danger and action stoically, and prefers physical pleasures rather than intellectual pursuits. *A Farewell To Arms* brings forth this creation of the "Hemingway Code" in Frederic Henry; he has also been looked upon by foreign critics as a personification of the American man. Undoubtedly, part of Hemingway's popularity as a result of *A Farewell To Arms,* even in the United States, was due to the impression that he represented the American "he man" who scorned sophistication and preferred nature. Because of the public's identification of Hemingway's own war service with that of Frederic Henry and his advocacy of the elemental and simple life of the outdoors and companionship, Hemingway helped in *A Farewell To Arms* to associate the man, the writer, and the legend.

ARTISTRY: Hemingway, contrary to some aspects of the myth, was a hard-working and conscientious literary artist. Starting *A Farewell To Arms* in Paris in March, 1928, he worked later in the year on the book in Florida, and finished the first draft in Wyoming during the same summer. It is rumored that he rewrote the conclusion seventeen times, and he stated not too long before his death that the ending still provoked sorrow in him. He also revised the galleys up to the last minute. It is also said that he spent six months in the composition of the novel and another five months in revisions. Critics have probed the skillful artistry shown in *A Farewell To Arms* and have found that it resembles a drama in five acts. It is the only one of Hemingway's novels to have been produced for the stage; and it has been made into movie versions on two occasions.

LIMITATIONS: Because of Hemingway's avoidance of complexity in style and ideas, his art has been criticized for being an "art of evasion," and at times the flight of the Hemingway hero from the complexities of existence produces a very slight aesthetic doctrine. The repetitious monotony of the vocabulary is certainly not admirable on many occasions, and the charge of escapism on the part of his heroes is difficult to answer. It must be also admitted that these are not only deliberate limitations by Hemingway, they are an intrinsic weakness of his own art. Within his artistic and philosophical limitations, Hemingway worked well; he was certainly a prolific reader, more so than was at first suspected by the critics. However, the avoidance of profound thought by his characters and their consequent reliance upon action and activity cannot be always upheld as the only possible solution for life's problems. Nor can Hemingway's insistence on "manhood" be regarded as a substitute for thoughtful decisions. In reading Hemingway, one must analyze the strengths and the weaknesses of this major American writer who deeply influenced his own countrymen and foreign authors as well.

BOOK ONE

CHARACTER ANALYSES

FREDERIC HENRY: Frederic Henry is the "hero" of the novel and the main character throughout the book. The story is narrated in the first person; with the exception of some use of "we" to denote his identity with other soldiers, the plot is developed from the point of view of "I." However, it must be kept in mind that Frederic Henry is a "Hemingway Hero." There is undoubtedly an autobiographical aspect to the literary creation of Frederic Henry. Hemingway, having volunteered and having been rejected because of an eye injury for the American Army, enlisted in early 1918 as an ambulance driver with the Italian forces. Shortly after his arrival in Milan, Hemingway experienced the hardships of war at first hand: the explosion of an ammunition plant in the city caused many casualties, and the young man of nineteen aided in the disaster. When he was sent to the front, Hemingway insisted upon being close to the trenches; he handed out Red Cross supplies to the Italian soldiers until he was wounded on July 8, 1918. His experiences resemble those of Frederic Henry in the first book of the novel. Hemingway, like his hero, also spent a long period in hospitals, where he underwent twelve operations. He returned to the war, fought with the infantry, and won two decorations from the Italian government. The battle scenes, so strikingly executed in *A Farewell To Arms,* are perhaps the best elements of the book; Hemingway is certainly writing from a sure and painfully gained knowledge.

FREDERIC HENRY AS AN IDEAL: It is impossible to separate the fictional from the factual in the literary analysis of Frederic Henry. He not only represents the young Hemingway but probably represents the youth of America who searched for idealism and objectives in a world torn by war.

FREDERIC HENRY'S SEARCH: The young man is searching for values in the war.

FREDERIC HENRY'S SPEECH: The style of speech of Frederic Henry is noteworthy. Indeed, the style of the entire novel is terse and economical, and the critics have had a field day praising and condemning the stylistic efforts of Ernest Hemingway. When Hemingway was awarded the Nobel Prize for literature in 1954, the citation called attention to his "forceful and style-making mastery of the art of modern narration." Frederic Henry is never unmasked in descriptions and this omission of physical and personality traits is one of the contributions of the Hemingway style. The characters are indicated through the dialogue; they are never shown in full light, only in shades and shadows. It is the responsibility of the reader to uncover the significance of the actors on the Hemingway stage. In the first book of *A Farewell To Arms,* Frederic Henry is characterized by an almost monosyllabic tone. Even in the crucial meeting with the priest in the hospital, he talks in short, concise sentences. Little is known of Henry's family; it is conveyed in Book One that he is estranged in some way from them by mention of the sight draft for money which will be honored by the family. Some critics have argued that the tone of the novel is set within the first book by Henry's laconic style: he has abandoned abstractions and noble phrases because of disillusionment with the war. Fearful of rhetorical devices which have served to lure youth into fighting for empty phrases, Henry only speaks with words he can clearly understand. He does not want to confuse or to be confused.

Henry's relations with Rinaldi are paralleled by his contact with the priest. The symbolism of these friendships has been established and is quite evident. The priest represents the effort to maintain religious and spiritual values in a world at war; he has hopes of instilling some of these attitudes in his companions, particularly Frederic Henry. Rinaldi is at the opposite end of the scale of values and it is no coincidence that Hemingway notes that the Italian officer is a surgeon. The contrast between priest and surgeon, religion and science, believer and nonbeliever, is very obvious. Despite a surface vulgarity, Rinaldi, like the priest, is fundamentally a good man, and Henry is cognizant of this goodness. Hemingway undoubtedly placed these chapters one after the other, ten and eleven, the visits of Rinaldi and the priest, in order to compare and contrast the two viewpoints. At the conclusion of the interviews, Frederic Henry is torn between the realistic, crude world of Rinaldi and the glimmer of hope that the priest expresses.

CATHERINE BARKLEY: Catherine Barkley plays a comparatively minor role in Book One of *A Farewell To Arms*. The few encounters with Catherine Barkley in Book One have not led to the creation of a strong character whose will struggles for expression. Edmund Wilson has pointed out Hemingway's tendency to portray obedient females who easily accept male domination, and Carlos Baker finds that the heroines, although stable, are abstract.

HELEN FERGUSON: Helen Ferguson, a minor character throughout the novel, is introduced briefly in this first book. In a sense, she might be considered the counterpart of Rinaldi although the latter has made an important contribution to the plot development so far.

COMMENT

FIRST BOOK: In the first book of *A Farewell To Arms,* the war is the principal theme. There are the descriptions of the landscape, the towns, and the troops in general. In this first part, there are no lengthy descriptions of battles and military strategy because Hemingway concentrates on the very personal reactions of the hero to the campaigns. Thus, the war is depicted in terms of the comfort and suffering of Frederic Henry. This is not a selfish view, however, because the American lieutenant is attentive to the feelings of the common soldiers. He suffers along with them and Hemingway creates the total impression of war-weariness.

WAR: The war is nothing glorious; in fact, boredom and monotony are characteristics of the Italian front noted in the first twelve chapters. Until Chapter IX, the war is ever-present but not immediate. In Chapter IX, significantly a very long chapter, the meaning of war is brought sharply into focus. It is one of the major episodes of the novel and illustrates why the book is primarily a war book and not a love story. Frederic Henry no longer remains a somewhat detached observer; he is now intimately involved. Thus, the war, in Book One of *A Farewell To Arms,* is studied from an angle of detachment so that it is omnipresent but deadening in its stillness; from the direct participation of the hero in front-line action and the consequent wounding; and finally from the reaction to fighting, in the vision of the wounded and dying in hospitals. Hemingway has also prepared with outstanding mastery the deeper insight into war he will portray later in the novel. In short, the war has no glorious, heroic, and idealistic traits; the war is a cruel, incomprehensible, and disillusioning way of life.

LOVE: The love story is merely introduced in the first twelve chapters; the war so overpowers all other considerations that meetings between lovers are brief, subject to cancellation, and generally unplanned.

SYMBOLISM: One of the most frequent symbols in the novel is that of the mountain and the plain; the mountain signifies the good and the plain the bad, according to Carlos Baker. This critic states: *"A Farewell To Arms* is entirely and even exclusively acceptable as a naturalistic narrative of what happened. To read it only as such, however, is to miss the controlling symbolism: the deep central antithesis between the image of life and home (the mountain) and the image of war and death (the plain)."

During the Fascist regime of Benito Mussolini, the book was banned in Italy, not for any slights against the Italian people, but because the Fascists believed that the novel instilled pacifist feelings in the populace. It depicted military defeats instead of victories.

In Book One, the reader must keep his attention centered on the development of the hero. One critic, Earl Rovit, has affirmed that "the total effect of the story depends on the degree of Frederic's self-realization or acceptance of the implicit meanings in his experience; for, as we have seen with Hemingway, the identity of a man is measured by the progressive recognitions of his meaningful experience." In his search for manhood in the twelve chapters, Henry has come into contact with the cynical realism of Rinaldi, the subtle idealism of the priest, and the personal sufferings of war. Sex is an apparent palliative in this quest for maturity; love is the goal which the priest advocated. Thus, in Book One, the major characters have been presented, and the love affair, overshadowed by the war as the dominant motif, has entered to disrupt the existence of Frederic Henry and Catherine Barkley.

BOOK TWO

CHARACTER ANALYSES

FREDERIC HENRY: Frederic Henry in the second book of *A Farewell To Arms* undergoes an important change in his personality and attitude toward life. Hemingway has received recognition in recent criticism as a very careful craftsman. It is said that he rewrote the book's conclusion seventeen times. Therefore, the differences and changes in Frederic Henry's character should be carefully noticed in the initial and final two chapters of Book Two.

CATHERINE BARKLEY: Catherine Barkley undergoes no fundamental change in character in the second book of *A Farewell To Arms*. Her prosaic personality has been severely ridiculed by critics, such as Edmund Wilson and Malcolm Cowley. Stewart Sanderson writes that "she is too highly idealised, the romantic vision of an adolescent's erotic daydream; the relationship between her and Frederic is altogether too smooth and perfect to be true." Although this critic modifies his judgment later in the text, the critique is quite typical of unacceptance of the Hemingway heroine. Nevertheless, Catherine Barkley forms an interesting comparison and contrast with the hero. It must be kept in mind, also, that Hemingway has centered his novelistic art on the development of Frederic Henry and not Catherine Barkley. He dominates each of the five books of the novel; he is in the vortex of the action during Book Three, and Catherine plays no part in the third section.

Keeping in mind, therefore, this intention of Hemingway and his known preoccupation with the male rather than the female protagonists of his novels, the balancing of Frederic and Catherine seems to be skillfully executed. Frederic is realistic, and Catherine is romantic. In many ways, the girl is in love with love itself.

CATHERINE'S PREGNANCY: In Chapter XIX, the symbol of the rain is used to convey her fright; she is unsure of herself in rainy, damp, and windy weather. Thus, when Hemingway notes the condition of the day, there is an indirect indication of Catherine's mood.

MINOR CHARACTERS: The three doctors, who are incompetent and dour individuals, contrast sharply with Valentini, the lively, skillful surgeon. Hemingway is probably indicating, as in other works, that those who are most human, sincere, and kind are also the most reliable in providing care and treatment.

Mr. and Mrs. Meyers, Ettore Moretti, and Ralph Simmons, as well as various other persons, some of them nameless, provide a light and frivolous side to the serious love story developed in Book Two. They are quite removed from the war and its consequences, except for Moretti, the braggart. These characters have not really lived and experienced; therefore, they contribute nothing to the unfolding of the personalities of Frederic and Catherine. It is a rather common device in Hemingway to introduce characters who are extraneous to the plot and characters; in other words, not every person must be judged as vital to a comprehension of the main drift of the story.

COMMENT

SECOND BOOK: Hemingway has now inverted his themes in terms of importance and emphasis. In Book One, the war overshadowed the nascent love affair between Frederic and Catherine; in Book Two, the love story comes to the fore, and the war is never directly inserted in the text. The war is restricted to the scenes in the military hospital, comments on military progress, and the inevitable meetings with combat personnel, such as Moretti and the nameless British major. However, the war is an omnipresent motif as the summer yields to the fall and Frederic's convalescence is completed. It is part of Hemingway's technique to have the lovers omit from their frequent conversations mention of this separating force; it is also forceful technique for Hemingway to conclude this part with a scene on the train, so characteristic of the episodes in the first book. Hemingway thereby indicates clearly that the war is returning in the coming book to occupy the reader's main attention.

LOVE: Thus, the theme of love reaches its apex in Book Two. Both characters find that love unites against the blows of life, and the two, even at the departure, are prepared to accept the consequences of their commitment to this ideal. Slowly, as the second part comes to its conclusion, disaster looms more immediate. Part of the great interest in the developing love motif is in the dialogue between the two; there are no descriptions of the physical action and no psychological probing. The form is made highly dramatic by this use of dialogue; in fact, *A Farewell To Arms* was adapted to theatrical presentation in the early nineteen thirties. It is the only novel of Hemingway's to find its way to the stage.

STYLE: The conversations between the lovers are generally indicated by the concise, simple language usual in Hemingway and noted in Book One. Neither of the two speaks at great length; often one line represents the speech of each person. The language is indicative of the speaker and his attendant personality; for example, Catherine uses the word "darling" very frequently throughout the chapters. The language of Frederic tends to be less lively and exuberant than that of Catherine; it may also be the reflection of the stoic attitude which Hemingway gives his hero. Consequently, there are really no tensions built up between the lovers; indeed, this aspect is one of the criticisms of Edmund Wilson, Malcolm Cowley, and others. Hemingway, these critics claim, never gets the relationship off the ground; the lovers are still living an idyllic existence and do not engage in the daily exchange of agreement and disagreement. Even in their agony and tragedy, brought to the surface as Book Two unfolds, they really do not partake in a meaningful dialogue.

SYMBOLISM: Hemingway continues to employ a repeated symbolism as in the first book. In this part, Hemingway employs the recurrent contrast of summer and autumn, and the rain. The love affair blossoms during the fateful summer in Milan, and the author inaugurates Chapter XVIII, the beginning of the idyll, with the statement that they had a wonderful experience during that summer. Since it is the summer, and so many of these enjoyable times take place out-of-doors, the weather is in favor of the lovers' trysts. Occasionally, the rain interferes with their pleasures, and it is significant that Catherine fears the rain. As the summer turns to fall and the rains increase, the symbolic use of the seasons and the weather is joined together. Then, the rain will take on added meaning: it will become synonymous with death, an inevitable thought as Frederic's leave expires.

Finally, in the last two chapters, there is an able employment of the symbols: the autumn with rainy weather becomes associated with the sadness of parting, the impending doom, and death. Also, illicit love is indicated by rain, and Catherine dwells upon this thought when rainy weather intervenes. She has more preoccupations about their immoral state in bad weather; in good weather, she believes that they are already sanctified except for the formal church bonds. In short, the rain denotes evil, war, and sin; whenever Hemingway wishes to convey these impressions, he conveniently gives the reader a spell of foul weather. Carlos Baker, who has studied in great detail the symbolism of Hemingway, insists upon this interpretation, but it is important to bear in mind that there is opposition to this opinion. E. M. Halliday is emphatic in opposing this viewpoint; he believes that Baker has overstated his case. He is pointed in his rebuttal: "What all this illustrates, it seems to me, is that Mr. Baker has allowed an excellent insight into Hemingway's imagery and acute sense of natural metonymy to turn into an interesting but greatly overelaborated critical gimmick." However, Carlos Baker is just as insistent on the importance of symbolism in *A Farewell To Arms*: "Once the reader has become aware of what Hemingway is doing in those parts of his work which lie below the surface, he is likely to find symbols operating elsewhere." These divergent points of view are important to remember and, during the reading of the novel, the reader should try to determine for himself the extent of symbolism in the book. The fact that two critics can disagree so visibly on this matter illustrates that *A Farewell To Arms* bears a very careful study.

BOOK THREE

THE RETREAT: Hemingway has certainly not exaggerated the extent of the Italian collapse, and the defeat at Caporetto represents a terrible military disaster for Italy and for the Allies.

Hemingway never states bluntly how Frederic Henry is changing; the variations in his hero come about subtly but surely. In other words, Hemingway indulges in understatement which allows the reader to grasp the meaning through the simple and repeated vocabulary. Harry Levin, analyzing Hemingway's style, concludes that "it remained for Hemingway—along with Anderson—to identify himself wholly with the lives he wrote about, not so much entering into them as allowing them to take possession of him, and accepting—along with their sensibilities and perceptions—the limitations of their point of view and the limits of their range of expression." Thus, Hemingway identifies himself completely with the characters, particularly the "Hemingway Hero," so that the reader in turn accepts easily that he is closely associated with the adventures and trials of the protagonist. Harry Levin continues in his deductions about Hemingway's methods that "we need make no word-count to be sure that his literary vocabulary, with foreign and technical exceptions, consists of relatively few and short words. The corollary, of course, is that every word sees a good deal of hard use. Furthermore, his syntax is informal to the point of fluidity, simplifying as far as possible the already simple system of English inflections." Part of the ease of identification is consequently effected by this simple and repetitious use of words.

FREDERIC'S DESERTION: Malcolm Cowley asserts that "when Frederic Henry dives into the flooded Tagliamento, in *A Farewell To Arms,* he is performing a rite of baptism that prepares us for the new life he is about to lead as a deserter from the Italian army." Carlos Baker finds again the familiar symbol of the rain, this time in the form of water, as indicative of a change in Frederic's character. It is virtually impossible to say what Hemingway intended: whether or not a deliberately symbolic act is depicted or whether it happens as part of the realistic frame in which a river is Frederic's best means of escape.

HIS ANGUISH: In the two brief chapters concluding Book Three, there is one of the few extensive passages of stream-of-consciousness and lack of dialogue to convey mental impressions and psychological attitudes.

ESCAPE: In this concluding idea of Book Three, much of the Hemingway credo is to be understood. The decision of Frederic Henry has been built up gradually and logically but it has not been thought through to its full implications. Earl Rovit deduces that Hemingway "leaves the significant facts in the narrative structure; they are there because the narrator Frederic has abstracted them from the actor Frederic's experience. And these tell us that Frederic does not return to the Rinaldi position where there is nothing but emptiness and dryness underneath; nor does he embrace the faith of the priest. He accepts the reality of the naturalistic world in which death is a fact every bit as real as sex; but he also accepts the reality of a love which he helped to create, and this fact is also as real as death." The significance of the title, *A Farewell To Arms,* is probably due to this abandonment of a military career by Frederic Henry. Certainly in this section, he has passed through several interesting facets of spiritual growth and development.

OTHER CHARACTERS: In Book Three, Frederic Henry is the only character sketched in detail. Catherine Barkley, the heroine, does not appear at all. Rinaldi adds little or nothing to the portrait painted previously.

The various soldiers and civilians with whom the hero comes into contact are all caught up in a terrible tragedy. Good or bad, all of them struggle in various ways to save their lives. The main problem which all the minor characters face is that of immediate death. Even the fear of death, as observed when the word "Germans" is sounded, causes them to react abnormally. Hemingway is writing sharply and vividly of the little men and women enmeshed in the vortex of senseless and cruel war. In fact, most of the time Hemingway does not even bother to record the names of the soldiers. Piani, Aymo, Bonello are named because they are the ambulance helpers, and Henry has to address them separately. Otherwise, there is a vast anonymity cast over the characters in the great retreat from Caporetto; this anonymity adds to the pathos of these individuals caught in a net not of their own making.

COMMENT

THIRD BOOK: The outstanding theme in *A Farewell To Arms* is war, which is brought to the fore in this third book. For that reason, it has been compared to Leo Tolstoy's *War and Peace,* particularly for the resemblance to the retreat from Moscow of Napoleon in 1812. The novel has achieved status with Erich Maria Remarque's *All Quiet on the Western Front* as one of the most important books dealing with World War I. Although the love story overshadows the war motif in the total framework of the novel, Book Three is devoted exclusively to the martial aspect. In fact, much of the fame Hemingway gained from this book is due to his masterly and accurate rendition of the sights and sounds of battle. Stewart Sanderson writes: "Hemingway's highly developed interest in military matters, which brought him back to Spain in the Civil War and to France at the head of an irregular fighting unit in the second World War, is mirrored in the accounts of the fighting on the Italian front. The descriptions of conditions in the lines, the troops and equipment and field dressing stations, are perfectly realised reportage, presented with a highly selective eye for telling detail. But there are other aspects of his writing about the war which concern us here. The emotional reactions to the facts of trench warfare, the attacks and retreats, the shelling and the casualties, the gap between the words and the realities of courage and victory and honor, are carefully analyzed and re-created." However, Hemingway never goes into the strategy of the overall campaign; there is no indication of the exact details of the Caporetto retreat in precise military terms. The reader is never told exactly when the attack started; at what sector the offensive was launched; and the effect produced for the Allied or Italian cause. The author does, nevertheless, give the small items of the debacle as it affected Frederic Henry and the common soldiers caught in the campaign. This emphasis upon the results of war as it involves the individual and the civilian is certainly one of the noteworthy contributions of Hemingway in *A Farewell To Arms*. In this regard, he has made the war seem very personal; the reader comprehends the plight of the soldier, who might very well be himself, in the detailed and selective manner of Hemingway. By choosing to depict not a victorious episode but a military defeat, and especially a disastrous retreat, Hemingway has shown the utter folly of war and the breakdown of men under its strains. The lieutenant-colonel, who is arrested and shot by the military police at the same time Frederic is arrested, is not a coward. In one vignette, Hemingway has summed up his doctrine of the "Hemingway Hero," that stoical, fundamentally courageous individual, as well as the idea of war's absurdity.

SYMBOLISM: Also in Book Three, the weather is emphasized as part and parcel of the elements acting against Frederic Henry. Although it is perilous to explore how deeply symbolic all this mention of "rain" and "water" is, it is probably no coincidence that Hemingway has employed this technical device in the Third Book.

THE "HEMINGWAY HERO": Finally, one must keep in mind how the "Hemingway Hero" is formed by adversity and hardship, although there is the inevitable breaking point. A critic said that "for Hemingway life is inseparable from death and is a fight at close quarters in which his heroes overcome not only the fear of death but the fear of life's intricacies and the disintegration threatening the individual. It is real life, work, and creative power that give him strength for the fight." This critic, Ivan Kashkeen, finds in this idea the pattern of being "alive in the midst of death," not only for the heroes of Hemingway but also in the life of the author.

BOOK FOUR

CHARACTER ANALYSES

FREDERIC HENRY: Frederic Henry accepts his course of action in this book; there are no radical changes in his mood and personality but rather a deepening sense of obligation and appreciation. Thus, Earl Rovit writes: "in Book Four, Frederic's course is confirmed. Moved by circumstances beyond his control, he accepts the consequences of his forced actions, among them the obligations of *caring* for Catherine in the priest's sense."

FREDERIC'S STOICISM: Malcolm Cowley analyzes this power of Hemingway to evoke the hidden depths of man: "And it is this instinct for legends, for sacraments, for rituals, for symbols appealing to buried hopes and fears, that helps to explain the power of Hemingway's work and his vast superiority over his imitators. The imitators have learned all his mannerisms as a writer, and in some cases they can tell a story even better than Hemingway himself; but they tell only the story; they communicate with the reader on only one level of experience." Thus, there is a more profound aspect to Hemingway's work than the surface simplicity of vocabulary and syntax would indicate; Hemingway is really digging deep into the subconscious of his characters, and Cowley concludes that ". . . most of us are also primitive in a sense, for all the machinery that surrounds our lives. We have our private rituals, our little superstitions, our symbols and fears and nightmares; and Hemingway reminds us unconsciously of the hidden worlds in which we live."

Ray West dissects him in this manner: "Frederic is the modern hero, lost between two worlds, the world of tradition and certainty which he cannot wholly relinquish, and the exciting but uncertain world of the twentieth century, where you only occasionally find something substantial to look at to make everything stop whirling, where you live for the moment, giving yourself up to sensations, for it is through the senses that you discover truth."

SWITZERLAND: Logically again, the hero of Hemingway expresses the fact that he is a man of action by his mammoth breakfast; the satisfaction of hunger and thirst is the basic clue to the contentment of the hero. It is interesting to notice how often the hero will drink and enjoy liquor as a sign of his joy of life. Carlos Baker sees in this exhilarated mood of Frederic Henry in Switzerland the resurgent imagery of the mountains as a source of strength and contentment. E. M. Halliday is less insistent on this specific interpretation and generalizes that ". . . it is undeniable that in the midst of the darkling plain of struggle and flight which was the war in Italy, Frederic Henry thinks of the Swiss Alps as a neutral refuge of peace and happiness—surely millions must have lifted their eyes to those mountains with like thoughts during both World Wars."

CATHERINE BARKLEY'S LOVE: Catherine Barkley, reappearing in Chapter XXXIV after a long absence, has suffered no change and has really not altered in her surrender of personality to her lover. This is why various critics insist upon the basic weakness of presentation of the heroines in Hemingway. Prior to the Caporetto fiasco, Catherine, always subordinated to interest in Frederic, nevertheless needed to be known and analyzed. Now there is no change; in fact, she no longer expresses her own evident worries and stresses to Frederic. It is doubtful whether the complete disavowal of individuality on Catherine's part can be fully justified. Leslie Fieldler has gone to the extreme of forecasting a dire and bleak future for the union between Frederic and Catherine: "Had Catherine lived, she could only have turned into a bitch; for this is the fate in Hemingway's imagination of all Anglo-Saxon women."

Hemingway has sketched a very romantic heroine who is an ideal mate; unfortunately, it is difficult to accept this standard as a realistic portrayal in view of the difficulties, especially the pregnancy, which Catherine is undergoing in Book Four.

COUNT GREFFI: Count Greffi is the most interesting of the minor characters and his role resembles somewhat that of Rinaldi and the priest. His air of dignity symbolizes an age which has ended with the outbreak of World War I. Of more importance, he provides justification to Frederic of the religious nature of love. It is interesting that Hemingway has selected a member of the nobility as one of the most sympathetic and important minor characters in the novel; usually, the author concentrates his sympathies with the common folk and depicts unfavorably those individuals in higher social classes.

MINOR CHARACTERS: All the Italian common people represent the deep-seated resentment and bitterness against the war among the Italians. The impression is conveyed that these poor and humble people have been deceived by the politicians and the generals—and are beginning to be aware of their plight. In Book Four, none of these individuals is "bad" in the Hemingway code; they are all "good" persons who are frantically struggling to survive the holocaust. Certainly no charge of anti-Italian bias can be leveled at Hemingway in *A Farewell To Arms,* as was attempted by some nationalistic critics. Mario Praz of the University of Rome has traced the literary fortune and influence of Hemingway in Italy. He notes in his study that Hemingway was known, respected, and imitated despite the Fascist ban on his works for almost twenty years. On the contrary, Hemingway feels sorry for the tragic situation of the people trapped in a bad strategic gamble.

The same comment may apply in part to Hemingway's depiction of the Swiss toward the end of Book Four. He is following the commonly accepted cliché that the Swiss are practical people who have preserved their way of life in the midst of war by providing comfortable service. The fact that the Swiss lieutenant becomes more amiable when he learns of their finances and that the other officials suggest good hotels and pleasant accommodations is only a humorous example of Hemingway's art. The whole peaceful and optimistic air of the last few pages of Book Four contrasts acutely with the tragic qualities of the residence in Italy.

FOURTH BOOK

COMMENT

ITALIAN INTERLUDE: Book Four may be conveniently divided into two sections, the residence in Italy which contrasts with the military side in Book Two, and the initiation of the

Swiss stay. The trip by boat in rather uncertain weather connects the two distinctly different interludes and provides some suspense for the reader. Hemingway demonstrates again that he has carefully plotted his novel and has just as skillfully balanced the impressions he transmits to his reading audience.

Another justification may be sought in Henry's character; he is "caring" at times, still "not caring" at others. Thus, Earl Rovit writes that ". . . although Henry represses and ignores it for the most part, he does possess a strong potential 'caringness.' There are times, as we see in the excerpt, when he cares a good deal; and everything becomes 'sharp and hard and clear.'" The last few pages of the section are certainly the happiest pages for the lovers, and if Hemingway had wanted to give a thoroughly romantic conclusion to the story, he could have ended *A Farewell To Arms* with the last line of Part Four to the effect that Catherine and Henry "followed the boy with the bags into the hotel." Of course, this would have destroyed much of the effect built up throughout the four books about the power of life and death, and the whole brooding backdrop of the war.

FLIGHT FROM ITALY: Hemingway employs again the now familiar symbol of the rain: he writes in the very beginning of Chapter XXXVII, the escape to Switzerland, that the rain came only in brief intervals. In other words, the trip will evidently be successful with moments of peril. At Stresa, the rain comes on occasion; when it does, Henry becomes pensive. In Chapter XXXIV, he has one of the most reflective moods in the book during an especially rainy night when they are alone in the hotel. When the sunshine appears the next day, both Catherine and he are in a gay state of mind. The only time when the two believe that they have overcome the challenge of the world, the stepping ashore in Switzerland, the rain is considered to be "cheerful" and "fine." If the rain represents the "world" in Hemingway's and Frederic's vision, or the dark forces of fate as Carlos Baker declares, then the main characters have apparently triumphed, or believe they have. Of course, if victory were assured, the novel would have been terminated at this point of near-perfect happiness.

BOOK FIVE

CHARACTER ANALYSES

FREDERIC HENRY: He runs head-on to his destiny in Book Five of *A Farewell To Arms*. He must now live in the full glare of his shattering experience, and Earl Rovit writes: "Frederic Henry establishes a connection with the world in his love affair with Catherine and, in so doing, becomes humanly alive. That she dies does not negate his experience; it pushes him into the position of the Major who also had trouble in resigning himself." In Book Five, Henry basically suffers no character transformation; he has been formed in the first three books. In fact, Book Four only intensified these traits, which were formulated especially by the great retreat of Caporetto. Agony and trial come when ideals are brought to bear on specific problems. In this case, death is the ordeal to be mastered, and the theme of death is intrinsic in this novel. Death is likewise one of the dominant preoccupations in the whole opus of Ernest Hemingway.

APPARENT PEACE: There is a brilliant reversal of emphasis in Book Five because the reader has been led to fear the death of Frederic Henry in the war as the danger. The hero is plunged into the abyss of something perhaps worse: the death of Catherine, without whom he cannot have peace of mind.

He seeks no other company, no friends or social acquaintances; indeed, he cannot bear to be alone for too long. The reader is led to believe that Frederic Henry will survive and will endure; he has become a man of sensation, a man of action. He will wear the scars of his sufferings; he will be hardened and cynical; and he will expect death in any form and on any occasion to destroy his illusory security.

FREDERIC AS THE TOTAL "HEMINGWAY HERO": Frederic Henry comes to the full height of a "Hemingway Hero" in the final scenes at the hospital. He stoically challenges fate and loses, but he really does not break down. His visits to the hospital are interspersed with jaunts to the nearby café to eat. Some may interpret this as undue hardness and say that a man in such circumstances, especially as Catherine's condition deteriorates, would never be able to eat and drink at such a time. However, this is exactly the stance of the "Hemingway Hero." Frederic must be outwardly calm; he must accept the struggle with fate's offerings.

In Chapter XLI, the moment of truth arrives for Frederic; in a rather long paragraph of stream-of-consciousness, the possibilities of life or death are brought to the surface in a series of short sentences, often in the form of questions. Then, the import of his struggle with life is fully apparent: life is a "trap" which is baited with good fortune and some happiness until the fatal step into death.

He cannot be victorious in his journey through life but Frederic is not ready to die. He walks with burdens of grief and pessimism in the knowledge that these things signify the responsibility of being a man. Frederic Henry, however, is not only a man in his complete maturity; he is likewise the development of the "Hemingway Hero."

CATHERINE BARKLEY: Catherine Barkley comes full circle

in Book Five as her lover does. She always wanted to submerge her personality into his, and she proves her mettle in the death scene. Although criticism has been leveled at her weakness as a character, her death shows her as exemplifying the stoical doctrine of Hemingway. Unfortunately, these characteristics were not revealed in any depth previously.

CATHERINE'S DEVOTION AND SACRIFICE: One may consider that the personality of Catherine remains static prior to her entry into the hospital; in the last, long chapter, she exposes her fears and her reactions, which parallel those of her lover. In other words, she has sacrificed her own feelings for his tranquillity; at her moment of crisis, she shows that her personality has not only been surrendered for his sake but that her ideals are the same as his. Both have the same attitude toward life. Like Frederic, Catherine is physically brave, and this aspect is a fundamental one for the characters of Hemingway. Physical valor is the intrinsic and most evident quality of the "good" person in Hemingway's credo.

It is important to observe how closely Catherine's philosophy approximates that of Henry's in the last chapter. Of course, she is likewise the romantic heroine in the tragic Chapter XLI; the lengthy description of her agony and death is typical of the romantic tradition of the past. Her philosophy demonstrates Hemingway's departure from the melodramatic; the author has inserted a profound attitude toward life and death in his heroine which rescues Catherine from some of the adverse criticism in the other books of the novel.

MINOR CHARACTERS: The minor characters are completely subordinated to the tragedy which occurs to Frederic and Catherine. In fact, most of the characters are not even named; only the Guttingens receive that recognition. There is a cloud of anonymity cast over all the persons in Book Five; in these moments, no one can provide help or a solution for the lovers.

The reactions of the minor, nameless characters in Book Five reflect Hemingway's doctrine that outside society is uninterested in the struggles of others. For the author, this attitude is not of necessity bad; on the contrary, it emphasizes the aloneness of the hero and the solitary effort to achieve identity. In the confrontation with life and death, or the world, solitariness is the desired and inevitable attribute. For that reason, the Swiss, who appear in the last book, are "good"; they reflect what the "Hemingway Hero" must endure.

BOOK FIVE

COMMENT

THE HEMINGWAY CREDO: Book Five comes as an anticlimax to the novel, and it is evident that if Hemingway had wished a happy ending to his story, he would have concluded after Book Four. The last part had to be brief and dramatic. At the same time, Hemingway comes to full strength in the creation of his two characters and his philosophy. Ray West views the total effect as ironical and masterful: "His life with Catherine in Switzerland and the life which they anticipated after the war were relatively devoid of conflict. Catherine and Frederic had said farewell to the life of action and struggle, but ironically their greatest test—the attempt to save the life of Catherine—came at the very moment when they seemed to have achieved a successful escape." At the beginning, the happiness of the couple continues to be on the ascendancy; and the mountains and snow of Montreux reflect this optimistic feeling. Although E. M. Halliday cannot accept Carlos Baker's insistence upon the mountains as representing goodness and joy, and his critique is especially insistent on questioning if the mountains around Caporetto could ever be so interpreted, he admits that Hemingway seems to hint at this meaning here. For example, Montreux, in the whiteness of the snow and the high mountains, is the apex of the lovers' idyll. Even the pregnancy is going well, and Catherine is exuberantly gay and optimistic. Lausanne represents a descent in all ways: the move is made because the snow is turning to rain, the mountains are yielding to the plain, symbol of trouble and unhappiness, and the hospital is located in Lausanne. The symbolism is clearest at this point: the next step down in the lovers' fortunes comes when the rains increase, spring arrives, and the hospital residence begins.

Thus, there are three distinct parts in Book Five: each denotes a diminution of happiness for Frederic and Catherine. The scenes in Montreux and Lausanne, not including the hospital episode, are high tides in the love affair, although there are signs of trouble already in the residence in Lausanne. The third part is contained within the entire last chapter; this last chapter also is exactly half the length of Book Five. It has already been mentioned that Hemingway labored long and hard in the composition of *A Farewell To Arms;* recent criticism has focused its attention on the skill which he devoted to its composition. Stewart Sanderson praises "the closely-knit texture of the novel, and the complex structural organization which underlies and sustains its surface." Carlos Baker always calls attention to the technical arrangement of the novel and stresses that Hemingway planned his procedures with the utmost care. It is therefore interesting to bear in mind how he ordered the scenery and divisions of each book to effect the total impression.

UNITY OF STRUCTURE: Sanderson makes the point, which has been noted by other critics, that the tragedy has the artistic construction of a drama in five acts. The third act is the longest and most vital element in the determination of the play's outcome; the Caporetto episode is the key to Frederic's philosophical orientation. The war descriptions are certainly unforgettable. The first two books depict the conflict in the character of Frederic Henry; and the last two books show the apparent victory and then swift, inevitable defeat of the protagonist. The Hemingway preoccupation with death and tragedy is brought out in Book Five; the emotion is intense; and the dramatic quality is high.

SYMBOLISM OF TITLE: The meaning of the title is completely illustrated in Book Five. On the first level of meaning, *A Farewell To Arms* refers to the abandonment of war on Frederic Henry's part; this interpretation is very clear in the revulsion toward the conflict which the hero expressed in the first book. His reactions were intensified in the second book and reach the point of outburst in his desertion at the end of the third part. The war really plays no role in Book Five. The escape from Italy to Switzerland provides the excitement of Book Four but even this episode is in the background. The love affair returns to the front of the stage in the last two books. Therefore, a second critical judgment has been made about the significance of the novel's title which only can be fully understood in Book Five, and particularly, in Catherine's death. Frederic in the last lines of the novel states that his farewell to the dead Catherine was like a farewell to a statue. "Arms" may logically be assumed to refer to feminine arms, that is to say, the love of Catherine. She makes the plea to Frederic on the previous page not to share their love with other women he will have in his life. Both themes, war and love, have been the two forces around which Hemingway has constructed his novel. The war would seem to be the main thread, although critics differ on the degree of stress, and certainly the first thought that comes to mind in the word "arms" is the martial reference. In addition, the second interpretation needs the reading of Book Five.

There is an equally interesting third interpretation of the title.

One cannot make an armistice or a separate truce with life as Frederic Henry attempted to do with the war. His commitment must be total, and he must pay the price for winning manhood. According to critics such as Ray West, Earl Rovit, and others, the meaning of *A Farewell To Arms* is more profound and more symbolical than suspected when the novel was published in 1929. Not the war and not love but the development and passage of the "Hemingway Hero" through life and its perils are the prime elements of this book. Therefore, critical attention must follow the path of Frederic Henry as the axis around which flow the other currents of war and love. If one accepts this emphasis upon the central character rather than the themes of war and love, then the title refers ironically to the hero's tragic condition. As in the army, he has made a pact with his destiny and he cannot elude it. Only death will be the farewell that the hero can render to the human condition.

"ARMS" AS A THREE-FOLD IMAGE: Regardless of these three interpretations, and the three may be equally valid in lieu of any definitive statement from Hemingway, Book Five is highly important for the meaning of the novel. One cannot justify any statement that Hemingway only composed the fifth book for emotional catharsis or melodramatic effect. The novel is initiated on a tragic note, in the deaths of the soldiers, and in the threat of annihilation which hangs over humanity. In the last book, Hemingway has brought about a shift in the immediacy of death from the impersonal and gigantic to the personal and minute. The author wrote of war in general in the first chapter of the novel; he makes the wry and ironic observation that only seven thousand soldiers died of the cholera during the winter. By the end of Book Five, the reader is engrossed in the intimacy of Catherine's death and Frederic's loss, which has nothing to do with the outcome of the war and the terrible losses being suffered at that very time in the 1918 spring offensive of the Germans. The hero made a passing reference, shortly before Catherine enters the hospital, to this fact. Thus, Hemingway has brought life and death into clear and certain terms; he may even mean in Book Five that there is a farewell to war as the critical motif in man's anxieties and agonies. Harry Levin in his study of Hemingway's stylistic achievements praises this power to extract meaning from words: "This may help to explain why it suggests a more optimistic approach to language than the presumption that, since phrases can be snares and delusions, their scope should be limited to straight denotation. The powers of connotation, the possibilities of oblique suggestion and semantic association, are actually grasped by Hemingway as well as any writer of our time. Thus he can retrospectively endow a cheap and faded term like 'mashing' with all the promise and poetry of awakening manhood."

CHARACTER ANALYSES

FREDERIC HENRY: To the positive force of love is added the growing preoccupation about the meaning of life. Thus, in the first book, Frederic passes from an introduction to love to the blossoming of the emotion in Book Two. In Book One, he was still blissfully unaware of the meaning of being a man; in Book Two, he begins to glimpse maturity because of the engagement with love. Therefore, one can trace surely and logically the trajectory of Frederic Henry's course in the first two books: the orbits of love and manhood are closely bound together.

HEMINGWAY HERO: He is also beginning to develop more completely and more deeply the characteristics of the "Hemingway Hero." At the introduction of Frederic Henry into the story in Book One and at the insights already given in these early chapters, the model is established in some degree. Frederic Henry is laconic, speaks briefly, uses simple vocabulary and syntax, and is unswayed by grandiose claims to his better nature. In this connection, the interviews with Rinaldi and the priest are the most revelatory of Frederic Henry's inner moods and intrinsic personality. If his thoughts ever come to the surface up to this point, the evidences can probably be found in these incidents. With Catherine, the hero begins to reveal his true dimensions. There exists in his soul a dichotomy between the desire for identity and the rootless nothingness he has met; and Ray West writes: "at the beginning Frederic wavers between reason and sensibility, between formal religion and 'true' Christianity, between the empty forms of love and true love. He has been thrust into a world of violent action in which choice is eventually to become necessary . . . The Hemingway hero is, theoretically, passive, because he is allied to nature through his unreason, but his particular dilemma usually has all the appearances of active seeking." By the time Frederic returns to the war front at the end of Book Two, he has been faced with this new addition to his existence. He has still not formulated the doctrine of the "Hemingway Hero." Book Three is the baptism of fire of this "Hemingway Hero," and Frederic's preoccupations and changed moods are sharply pinpointed in his contacts with his comrades, Rinaldi and the priest. It is important to trace exactly and surely why the hero is altered and what is the concrete outline of his personality. Frederic Henry is placed in the midst of not only a great battle but a terrible defeat. Such an awesome event has a positive and a negative result: the sufferings and physical strain wear down the stamina of any person so engaged, as proved by the desertions, cowardice, and looting described by Hemingway, and create a breaking point at which no further service is rendered. At the same time, the foundations are laid for the "Hemingway Hero." In short, he will be a man not of contemplation but of action; he will devote himself to love, happiness, and the elementary pleasures of life, such as food and drink. Each day will be enjoyed to its fullest but no hedonistic philosophy is meant here. In the back of the hero's mind is the bitterly learned knowledge that life is a farce and is absurd. The hero must find Catherine to support him in his new dimensions; without her, he cannot accede to the tremendous demands put upon him by life, or, in Hemingway's terms, the "world." Malcolm Cowley thus defines the problem of the "Hemingway Hero" and his environment: "His heroes live in a world that is like a hostile forest, full of unseen dangers, not to mention the nightmares that haunt their sleep. Death spies on them from behind every tree. Their only chance of safety lies in the faithful observance of customs they invent for themselves." However, one should always look at the two sides of a coin; the present state of Frederic Henry and his fellows does not always gain unqualified admiration for Hemingway. For instance, Sean O'Faolain lampoons the type by saying of Hemingway: "his Hero is always as near as makes no matter to being brainless, has no past, no traditions, and no memories . . . We may regret this exclusive glorification of brute courage, strength, skill and grace, but I doubt if it is literary criticism to do so." Despite adverse criticism, the popularity of the "Hemingway Hero" has never been disputed; for example, Mario Praz and Deming Brown, after analyzing the impact of Hemingway in Italy and Russia respectively, conclude that he struck a chord not only in the general reading public but also within literary circles. Be that as it may, Frederic Henry and the other Hemingway types are realistically drawn and evoke sympathy and understanding.

IRONY: There is a widespread use of irony in Hemingway, as E. M. Halliday and other critics note, and this device is brilliantly exploited in the last two books of the novel. Here are the happiest interludes for Frederic Henry. He believes momentarily that he has avoided the consequences of his duties. The progress of love for Catherine has been successful and despite minor complications and forewarnings, all seems very bright. However, he is like a mouse approaching a trap, and it is interesting to note Hemingway's frequent use of animals as symbols for his heroes. When all the complications mount and intensify, Frederic Henry reaches his stature as a "Hemingway Hero." Shortly prior to Catherine's death and at the imminence of that sad event, Frederic realizes that once man is granted the boon of life (and it is a great gift, in Hemingway's belief), he must pay the toll. Death is the end of man and it must be faced; one must learn not only to live well but to die well. Man is alone, a tragic figure, haunted by his doom and condemned by a capricious destiny. Love is the bond which can unite men but it can be broken easily by fate. These are the lessons which

Frederic Henry has learned as he leaves the dead Catherine at the end; he faces the world stoically, sad and sobered by experience.

CATHERINE BARKLEY: Although Frederic Henry dominates the entire novel and Catherine never attains full development as a personality, she is the expression of love and the needed catharsis for her lover's spirit. Catherine plays no role and does not even appear in the crucial Book Three, the longest book of *A Farewell To Arms*. The analysis of this character must be sought on two levels: the changes in her prior to Caporetto and after Frederic's traumatic adventures in the disastrous retreat. She is in many ways the personification of the romantic heroine, prepared to devote herself, whatever the cost, to the ideal of love.

LOVE AS A DOMINANT IDEAL: Because of the lack of full psychological probing and depth of analysis, Hemingway has been often criticized by critics for his shallow treatment of the heroines in his novels.

Catherine is best depicted in the death scene. Then she makes a noteworthy contribution to the Hemingway doctrine about life and death and the world; she also provides a perfect complement to the attitude of Frederic Henry. Both have the same impressions: life is impossible to conquer and death is the ultimate end of the struggle. Catherine likewise expresses another key idea in Hemingway: physical courage and a stoical stance when faced by death. Hemingway, in the last chapter of Book Five, brings Catherine completely within the scope of a realistic creation. This does not mean she abandons her romanticism; on the contrary, she is prepared to sacrifice herself for love and make Frederic happy. However, in the last chapter, Catherine exposes her innermost thoughts and reactions, which were hidden except for some revelatory expianations in the first two books. Perhaps this is the high point of the dedication to Frederic on Catherine's side: union of thought, mood, and spirit.

MINOR CHARACTERS: There are four minor characters who are influential in the development of the main characters: Helen Ferguson, Rinaldi, the priest, and Count Greffi. Helen Ferguson really serves as a foil to Catherine Barkley; she represents the view of morality and society about the love affair. There is also a contradictory element in the nurse's situation: she condemns the lovers but is unconsciously envious of their love. Thus, she represents two reactions of society and the outside world: criticism at the defiance of convention and jealousy at the happiness of two lovers.

RINALDI: Rinaldi symbolizes the reactions of the Italian officer class and the intellectuals to the war. Despite his overt crudity, Rinaldi is very intelligent, but his better instincts have been drowned in the blood bath of the war. He has given up all belief in the meaning of life and finds a solution for his personal agonies and those of humanity in physical pleasures, cynicism, and sarcasm. In many ways, he will explain the European attitude after World War I and the defeatism rampant throughout Italy.

THE PRIEST: Both Rinaldi and the chaplain are clearly and logically compared; the two represent contrasting reactions to the war, one abandoning any idealism or faith, and the other fighting a losing struggle to follow a set doctrine.

COUNT GREFFI: Count Greffi is the third influential character if Helen Ferguson is excluded from the list; he certainly suggests a third possible solution, in addition to Rinaldi's and the priest's, for the dilemma of Frederic Henry. Count Greffi, the symbol of a past social and political order, is a humanist; he believes in the genteel tradition and stability through appreciation of life. Of the three Italians, Count Greffi would agree very closely with Frederic's general mood, although the medical officer, the priest, and the old nobleman have all made contributions to the hero's psychological frame of mind.

There are many minor characters who are often nameless; and Hemingway generally favors their pitiful situation. He has a basic humanity which describes and observes rather than judges. He neither condemns nor approves. Hemingway shows particular sympathy for the common soldier and, although some of the fighting men may be cowardly, he tries to understand them. His depiction of the Italians, soldiers and civilians, is very favorable and it is evident that Hemingway sees the war as an exploitation of these people. His people, including the Swiss, are generally the "little" people, endeavoring to live out their lives in the shadow of great events; seldom are their motivations very good or very bad. They are, on the contrary, generated by basic human drives, and are on the whole kind and helpful to the lovers, Frederic and Catherine.

QUESTIONS AND ANSWERS

1. Discuss the use of irony in *A Farewell To Arms.*

ANSWER: The ironic contrast is found in the initial situation of Frederic Henry in the war. He represents a realistic reaction to the lofty idealism of his generation at the conflict's start. He has seen through the slogans and catchwords which have lured the young men of his age to the battlefields. At the same time his personal life is quite comfortable, far better than the lot of the ordinary soldiers whom he pities. In the third book, his close escape from execution by the military police is certainly ironical; he has dodged death from the attacking Germans and has shot one of the sergeants for desertion. Now he is seized as a deserter at the moment when he believes himself to be safely within his own lines.

The happiness of Catherine and Frederic is ironical because it is so illusory. When she is taken to the hospital to bring life into the world, she meets death. The baby, cause of all their anxieties, is born dead; Frederic remarks on this irony in the novel's last chapter. Hemingway also uses very ironical language in his descriptions, as in his first chapter, when he writes that only seven thousand soldiers died of cholera. Finally, the war setting of *A Farewell To Arms* is ironic in the historical context: after fighting doggedly for two years in a slow conquest of the mountains, the Italians are routed swiftly and lose all their costly military gains within a short time in the German and Austrian offensive.

2. How does Hemingway treat the theme of death in the novel?

ANSWER: Death is one of the important elements in the construction of *A Farewell To Arms.* There is the impersonal and the personal portrayal of death: the war obviously brings death as an everyday occurrence and Frederic's assignment as an ambulance driver has made him observe killing in the course of duty. While he is disillusioned about life in general, he still feels himself in no danger. He reflects upon the relative safety of the Italian front and his own unexposed position as a noncombatant. His first change of feeling occurs when he is wounded; then he realizes the meaning of death more closely, especially when he is removed in one of his own ambulances. The dripping of blood from a wounded soldier above him has its effect on him. Finally, in the retreat from Caporetto, Frederic Henry sees death at close hand. He learns that he can die by accident if he strays too close to the Italian rear guard or is mistaken for a spy. Brushes with death in the course of war come for soldiers and civilians alike.

3. What is meant by the statement that Hemingway employs "the art of evasion"?

ANSWER: Hemingway does not indulge in lengthy geographical and psychological description. His style has been said to lack substance because of the avoidance of direct statements and description of emotions. Hemingway relies upon the reader to interpret his meaning and only provides clues by his use of nouns without any revealing adjectives, or simple verbs. Hemingway favors action, and facts are set down in rapid succession. Seldom does the hero expound on his feelings; he is unmoved to lyrical outbursts. Instead of seeking commitment to an ideal or a cause, the characters are content to do their job without pondering the reasons or the consequences. If the emphasis is upon facts and acts of the will, then there is no necessity for lengthy, philosophical digressions. A character may therefore be said to evade any requirement to let the reader in on the processes of his mind. The hero, as happens to Frederic Henry, may have suffered a surfeit of flowery rhetoric and empty phrases; he is therefore wary of instituting a technique with which he is disillusioned. Evasion may refer to the lack of introspective analysis and the failure to evolve a responsibility in the characters. It takes shape in the reliance upon dialogue, and the passing from one action to another in rapid succession like a motion picture setting. The characters evade engagements in order to satisfy their basic passions, such as eating, drinking, and sex—all of which are stressed in Hemingway's novels.

4. What is Hemingway's attitude toward religion in *A Farewell To Arms?*

ANSWER: Hemingway seems to say that while organized religion is not the solution of his hero's problem, nevertheless some of the tenets of Christianity may be followed with profit. Despite these rejections of religion, the lovers are religious in the sense of following the dictates of their consciences and looking upon love as the guiding motif of their lives. Some critics have written that Hemingway, in spite of his apparent naturalism, has thereby instilled a metaphysical yearning in the inquietudes of Frederic and Catherine.

5. How is Hemingway's concept of time and space depicted in *A Farewell To Arms?*

ANSWER: Hemingway ranges far afield in the novel to give the impression that locale has no bearing upon feeling and that man is the same in all places. There is no unity of place in this book: the setting changes from the Italian war front to Milan and finally to Switzerland. Within these broad areas, there are other changes of scenery which do not affect the hero and heroine. Weather may play a role, but basically geography does not, except for the mention of mountains and plains. Hemingway does not go into the minute details of the physical settings; the places are "good" or "bad" depending upon the attitude of the principal characters. The war front is bad because of the lovers' separation and the war peril; Milan is good because the two are together; and Switzerland is good because Frederic and Catherine are enjoying their happiest moments together there.

Time is concentrated in the present in Hemingway's novel; in fact, he uses the present tense a great deal within the pages of *A Farewell To Arms*. Little is known of the histories of Frederic and Catherine, and they do not reminisce about the time previous to loving each other. Likewise, little thought is given to the future. Both endeavor to live to the fullest in the present; perhaps this is an indication of the doom which is awaiting the lovers.

6. What is Hemingway's attitude toward war in *A Farewell To Arms?*

ANSWER: Hemingway has written one of the most vivid and realistic accounts of war in contemporary literature. There is no romantic or idealistic aspect to his portrayal of World War I; the conflict is an impersonal force which destroys and leads to the breakdown of rationality. Hemingway's sympathies are with the common soldier and not the generals and military commanders. He does not discuss strategy other than in terms of how the individual is caught in the trap of suffering and death at the hands of others. War brings out certain primitive instincts in man and often shows the worth of an individual. Hemingway is interested in the reactions of men facing death:

their bravery or their cowardice, their regard for their comrades, and their spontaneous actions in battle. Hemingway seems to find the link of friendship and understanding as a possible result of soldiers being in the same dangerous plight. He also appears aware of the effects on civilians and tries to show humanistic actions in moments of stress. Hemingway sketches a very sharp distinction between men at war and men at peace; war exposes men to various pressures which change them drastically, as happens with the hero, Rinaldi, and the priest. Men at peace do not comprehend the problems of those in battle, as Frederic learns from the civilians after his return.

CRITICAL COMMENTARY

INTRODUCTION: The standard edition of *A Farewell To Arms* is published by Charles Scribner's Sons, New York. The first edition was published by that company in 1929. Hemingway's fame had been established by the publication of his first important novel, *The Sun Also Rises,* three years earlier. However, the latter novel deals with events and people of the nineteen twenties who reflect the war atmosphere of *A Farewell To Arms.* It is perhaps easier to understand the characters and the issues of *The Sun Also Rises* by first reading *A Farewell To Arms;* the so-called "Lost Generation" of Gertrude Stein, who enormously encouraged Hemingway during his struggling years in Paris after World War I, is made more comprehensible if one analyzes beforehand *A Farewell To Arms.* There is a close connection in theme, technique, and point of view in the two novels.

Although *The Sun Also Rises* brought Hemingway artistic and critical recognition, *A Farewell To Arms* won for him popular and financial rewards. The book was an immediate best-seller, in serialized form, in book format, on the stage, and in the movies. Perhaps a contributing factor to this popularity might have been the adverse criticism it aroused from certain groups: it was banned in Boston for a time, Mussolini refused its circulation in Italy, and people criticized its laudatory rendition of illicit love. At that time, some of the love scenes were considered too bold for the printed page. In the reaction against war at the time of the novel's publication, it was conceded a major place as one of the great war novels, besides Leo Tolstoy's *War And Peace* and Erich Maria Remarque's *All Quiet On The Western Front*. Robert Penn Warren says: "*A Farewell To Arms* more than justified the early enthusiasm of the connoisseurs for Hemingway and extended his reputation from them to the public at large. Its great importance was at once acknowledged, and its great importance has survived through the changing fashions and interests of twenty years."

EARLY CRITICISM: After the initial and favorable reception of the novel, critics began to dissect the book to ascertain the roots of the Hemingway success. Emphasis was directed to his masterly use of the war theme, the accurate and detailed descriptions of an ignored episode of World War I; the love motif was added to the martial atmosphere, and the romantic and tragic affair appealed to mass audiences. Philip Young defends the twin employment of these topics in Hemingway: "However, the notion that love-making and war-making are 'superficial activities' finds me with no defense at all. I might just as well admit that I have been under the impression that sex and killing were, in the personal and social spheres, respectively, the foremost problems of our age, and had never questioned their validity as proper subject matter. I cannot change overnight, so let them go as regrettable preoccupations—probably more signs of Hemingway's adolescence, and my own."

It bears repeating that the Nobel Prize in literature for 1954 was awarded to Ernest Hemingway for the narrative skill of his writings. In other words, as shall be soon seen, critics had concentrated on style, symbolism, and ideas in later years; but the prime appeal of novels such as *A Farewell To Arms* was due to the interesting and human story it tells. However, not even this notice has reconciled some critics; Leon Edel makes a compelling point when he writes that "nevertheless the Swedish Academy has not been very brilliant, on the whole, in its choice of Nobel prize winners; the last, going back to the beginning of the century, is filled with forgotten names, redolent with omissions." Edel sharply criticizes Hemingway for what he calls "the art of evasion" in that the hero of Hemingway expresses everything in oversimplified language; everything which cannot be reduced to the ego and the will of the hero is eliminated from consideration.

The British critic, Wyndham Lewis, as early as 1934, attacked the hero of Hemingway as "a dull-witted, bovine, monosyllabic simpleton." Other foreign critics, such as Aldous Huxley, D. S. Savage, and Sean O'Faolain, have scorned Hemingway's creation as exalting the emotional force and the brutish nature of man; they decry the "anti-intellectualism" of Hemingway's characters and also of the author. In some cases, the author may be dissociated entirely from his literary creation, but this is not the situation with Ernest Hemingway. The "Hemingway Legend" was growing during the years after the writing of *A Farewell To Arms* and the natural curiosity to know more about the man was enhanced directly and indirectly by Hemingway. His travels to many lands, his personal life, particularly his marital woes and exuberant sprees, all added to the natural connection with his heroes. Action, excitement, and violence either appealed to critics or not, depending upon their own personal tastes and literary favorites. Robert Weeks, generally a defender of Hemingway, does not approve of this constant use of the primitive nature: "His characters go into battle, but never to the ballot box; they are constantly being tested but never in a social context. According to this view, raw physical courage is not only the supreme value in his fictive world but practically the only one."

PRESENT CRITICISM: The Hemingway bibliography is prodigious and is increasing at a fast pace each year, which may be proof that he was not as simple and elementary as some critics have claimed. Shortly before the Nobel Prize Award in 1954, a serious revaluation of Hemingway took place. It is impossible to date this new outlook exactly, but Professor

Carlos Baker of Princeton University is certainly one of the leaders of this challenging interpretation. This critic probes the hidden depths of Hemingway's symbolism; he concludes that Hemingway was a far more profound literary artist than has been suspected. Baker stresses the symbolic use of the mountains and the plains, and the rain, as emblematic of his literary form. Although E. M. Halliday rebukes Baker for unduly emphasizing symbolism where none may be intended, he agrees in large measure with the thesis that Hemingway has much to offer the serious literary student. Philip Young admits the primitivism of the Hemingway characters but finds an interior struggle going on in the mind and heart of the protagonists. The surface world is only the reflection of the inner stress and strain. Malcolm Cowley traced the use of ritual, sacraments, and legends as symbolical of the unnoticed substratum of Hemingway's thought and literary skill. Cowley writes that Hemingway ". . . has earned the right to be taken for what he is, with his great faults and greater virtues; with his narrowness, his power, his always open eyes, his stubborn, chip-on-the shoulder honesty, his nightmares, his rituals for escaping them, and his sense of an inner and an outer world that for twenty years were moving together toward the same disaster."

Although Hemingway's style was often noted as part of his originality, only comparatively recently have the critics sought to arrive at the implications and techniques of Hemingway. Harry Levin observes the stress upon the noun, very easy verbs, and the absence of the adjective; this critic admits the weakness of syntax and diction but praises Hemingway's ability to convey action. Hemingway achieves a "sequence of motion and fact" by means of his linguistic mannerisms. Thus, the increasing Hemingway criticism is attempting to focus on the inner meanings of the man, the technical qualities of his writing, and the work as a unit to be studied without reference to the man. More recent criticism had dealt with the structural approach to individual works in hope of finding more of the basis for Hemingway's achievement.

BIBLIOGRAPHY

ATKINS, JOHN A., *The Art of Ernest Hemingway,* London, 1952. (Emphasis upon the language and symbols).

BAKER, CARLOS, *Hemingway: The Writer as Artist,* Princeton, 1952. (The leading authority on Hemingway in a major study stressed the symbolism and stylistics of Hemingway).

BAKER, CARLOS, ed., *Hemingway and His Critics,* New York, 1961. (A survey of American and foreign criticism, scholarly and popular).

BAKER, CARLOS, ed., *Ernest Hemingway: Critiques of Four Major Novels,* New York, 1962. (A scholarly approach to a structural comparison of four works).

COOPERMAN, STANLEY, "Death and Cojones: Hemingway's *A Farewell to Arms." South Atlantic Quarterly,* LXIII, 85-92.

FENTON, CHARLES A., *The Apprenticeship of Ernest Hemingway,* New York, 1954. (Outstanding work on the formative years of Hemingway).

FIEDLER, LESLIE A., *Love and Death in the American Novel*, Cleveland, 1962. (A Freudian interpretation of the novels).

FORD, FORD MADOX, Introduction, *A Farewell to Arms*, Modern Library edition, New York, 1932. (Important for the early recognition accorded Hemingway by a contemporary novelist).

GELFANT, BLANCHE, "Language as a Moral Code in *A Farewell to Arms*." *Modern Fiction Studies*, IX, 173-176.

GERSTENBERGER, DONNA, "The Wasteland in *A Farewell to Arms*." *Modern Language Notes*, LXXVI, 24-25.

GLASSER, WILLIAM, "Hemingway's *A Farewell to Arms*." *Explicator*, XX, Item 18. (A brief view of the novel's basic structure).

HACKETT, FRANCIS, "Hemingway: *A Farewell to Arms*." *Saturday Review of Literature*, XXXII (Aug. 6, 1949), 32-33. (A popular account of the novel's appeal).

HALLIDAY, E. M., "Hemingway's Hero." *University of Chicago Magazine*, XLV (May, 1953), 10-14.

HALLIDAY, E. M., "Hemingway's Narrative Perspective." *Sewanee Review,* LX (Spring, 1952), 202-18.

LEWIS, WYNDHAM, *Men Without Art,* London, 1934, pp. 17-40. (One of the severest attacks on Hemingway as an important novelist; completely unfavorable to him).

MARCUS, FRED H., "*A Farewell to Arms*: The Impact of Irony and the Irrational." *English Journal,* LI, 527-535.

McALEER, JOHN J., "*A Farewell to Arms*: Frederic Henry's Rejected Passion." *Renascence,* XIV, 72-79, 89.

McCAFFERY, JOHN K. M., ed., *Ernest Hemingway, the Man and His Work,* Cleveland, 1950. (A detailed study stressing the connection betwen the man, the writer, and the legend).

ROVIT, EARL, *Ernest Hemingway,* New York, 1963.

RUSSELL, H. K., "The Catharsis in *A Farewell to Arms.*" *Modern Fiction Studies,* I (Aug., 1955), 25-30.

SANDERSON, STEWART, *Ernest Hemingway,* New York, 1961. (A brief summary and analysis of the major works).

SIMPSON, HERBERT, "The Problem of Structure in *A Farewell to Arms.*" *Forum* (*Houston*), IV, iv, 20-24.

WEEKS, ROBERT P., ed., *Hemingway*: *A Collection of Critical Essays,* Englewood, 1962. (Previously published essays on a variety of topics).

YOUNG, PHILIP, *Ernest Hemingway,* New York, 1952. (One of first works to emphasize Hemingway's symbolism and careful craftsmanship).

NOTES

NOTES

NOTES

NOTES